# CASA

# CAVALLI

# HOME

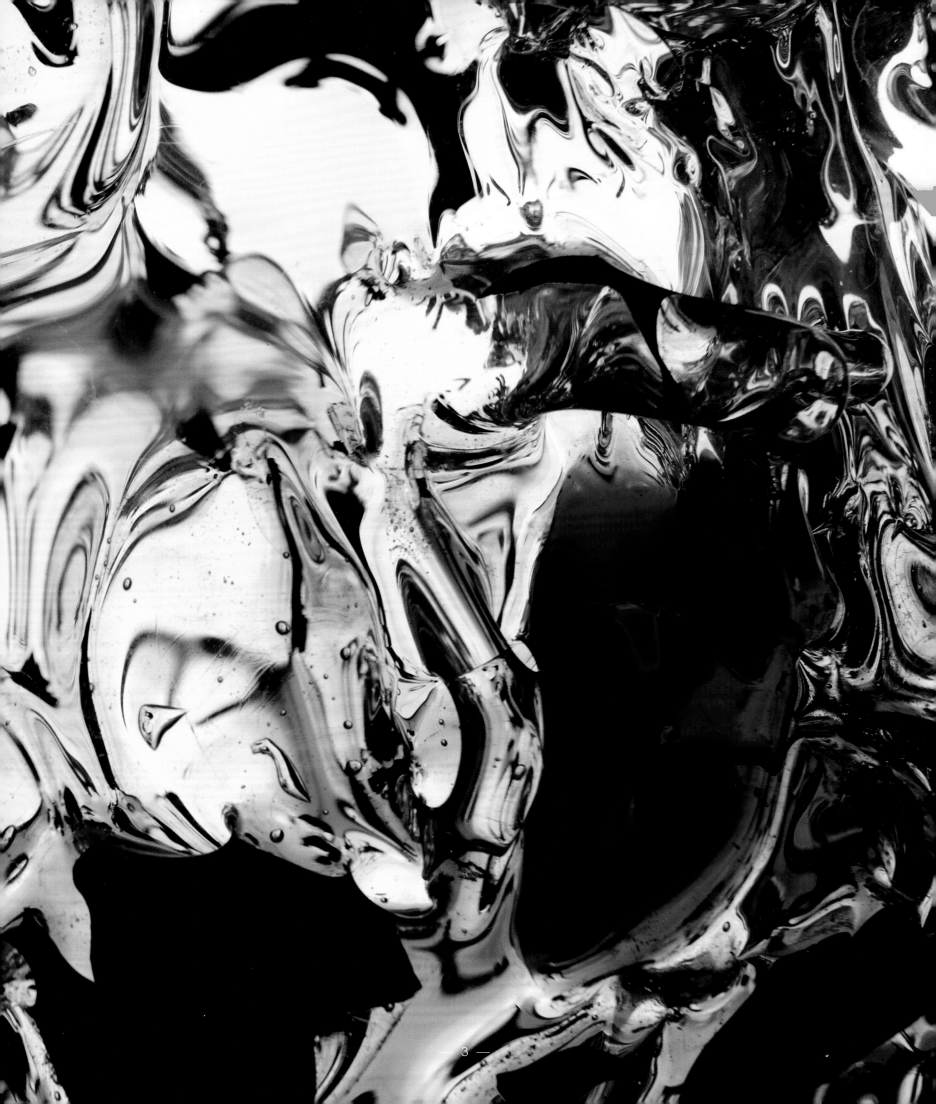

# CASA
# CAVALLI
# HOME

VENDOME

# WILD

OVER THE PAST FIFTY YEARS, ROBERTO CAVALLI HAS BECOME A GLOBAL FASHION AND LIFESTYLE POWERHOUSE, WITH SIGNATURE DESIGNS THAT HAVE DRESSED CELEBRITIES AND THE JET-SET THE WORLD OVER. IN 2012, THE COMPANY EXPANDED ITS LUXURIOUS SENSIBILITY TO INTERIORS, LAUNCHING ROBERTO CAVALLI HOME—THE DEDICATION TO BEAUTY AND UNAPOLOGETIC SENSUALITY FOR WHICH THE COMPANY HAS ALWAYS BEEN KNOWN NOW SHOWCASED HERE, IN THIS SUMPTUOUS VOLUME CELEBRATING THE HOME LINE'S FIRST TEN YEARS.

# GLAMOROUS

UNDER THE NEW CREATIVE DIRECTOR FAUSTO PUGLISI, THE COMPANY HAS INTRODUCED NEW LIMITED-EDITION PIECES ALONGSIDE THEIR ICONIC TABLEWARE, TILES, FURNITURE, LINENS, AND WALLPAPER. WHETHER GOLD-ENCRUSTED OR LEOPARD-SPOTTED, CAVALLI HAS BECOME A LIFESTYLE—ONE THAT IS INSTANTLY RECOGNIZABLE, THANKS TO THE BRAND'S COMMITMENT TO UNRIVALED QUALITY AND GORGEOUS PRINTS. THE STORY OF HOW THIS CAME TO BE BEGAN IN FLORENCE, WITH ROBERTO CAVALLI HIMSELF, THE "ARTIST OF FASHION" …

# EXUBERANT

# "I AM A CRAZY ARTIST."

Though born to a family of tailors in Florence, Roberto Cavalli initially followed his grandfather Giuseppe Rossi into painting. Rossi's early impressionistic canvases can be seen in the Uffizi Gallery, and his use of a light and dark patchwork to create scenes was of enormous influence on the young Cavalli, who took up studies at the local Art Institute of Porta Romana. But it was textile design that became the catalyst for his transformation from artist to fashion designer.

Initially, Cavalli started painting flowers on knits, which caught the eye of several producers. Following early successes, he continued to innovate, patenting a new method of leather *intarsio*—a patchwork technique similar to marquetry—created with dyed and printed leather, which appeared in Cavalli's first fashion show at the Paris Salon du Prêt-à-Porter in 1970.

By continuing to create new patterns—especially animal prints, jungle scenes, and other designs inspired by Cavalli's own photographs taken on safari and books on the natural world—and printing them on everything from silk to leather and denim, Roberto Cavalli has remained an innovative industry leader. Today, the Roberto Cavalli fashion house boasts a rich and storied archive of fabric prints, many of which were hand-painted by Roberto himself. With every new collection, these designs still inform each individual piece.

"La Stamperia—the printing house—
is my kingdom … La Stamperia is
the place where I get my hands dirty
with colors … where the anonymous
fabrics are embellished by
my colorful prints … where we
create your dreams with colors …
La Stamperia is the venue of one
of the most important steps:
the creation of each fabric,
so precious and unique that it
is destined to become a dress in
the Roberto Cavalli collection!"

ROBERTO CAVALLI

# IT IS IMPORTANT TO BE CHIC.

The process of translating elements of the fashion line into furniture, interiors, and *objets d'art* is realized with Cavalli's talented team in collaboration with artisans from across Italy. Through these partnerships with skilled craftsmen and women who have an inherited knowledge passed down through generations, Roberto Cavalli produces sumptuous, exquisite pieces that uphold the tenets of their "Made in Italy" certification. Brands like Roberto Cavalli remind us why Italy is a world leader in fashion and design.

At Cavalli's Tuscan glassworks, traditional techniques are used to hand-make crystal champagne flutes with gold engraving, while milky-white porcelain is detailed with animalier prints and floral motifs. Along Lake Como, the skilled hands of world-renowned weavers create stunning linens and tailored cloth robes, while in nearby Brianza exquisitely hewn chairs are sculpted and upholstered. This localized artisanship is what "Made in Italy" signifies, and the talented touch of Roberto Cavalli's production team, from the creation of porcelain tiles with wild spirit to spotted wallpapers studded with jewels, has the power to transform any room into a manifestation of glamorous elegance.

With Fausto Puglisi at the reins, new pieces are being created through the filter of fifty years of history, reinterpreting many of the company's classic animal prints with designs that have added a new spirit to Roberto Cavalli Home. And, as the company looks to the future, this iconic design empire with the power to animate any interior is now setting its sights on leading the field for the next fifty years—and beyond.

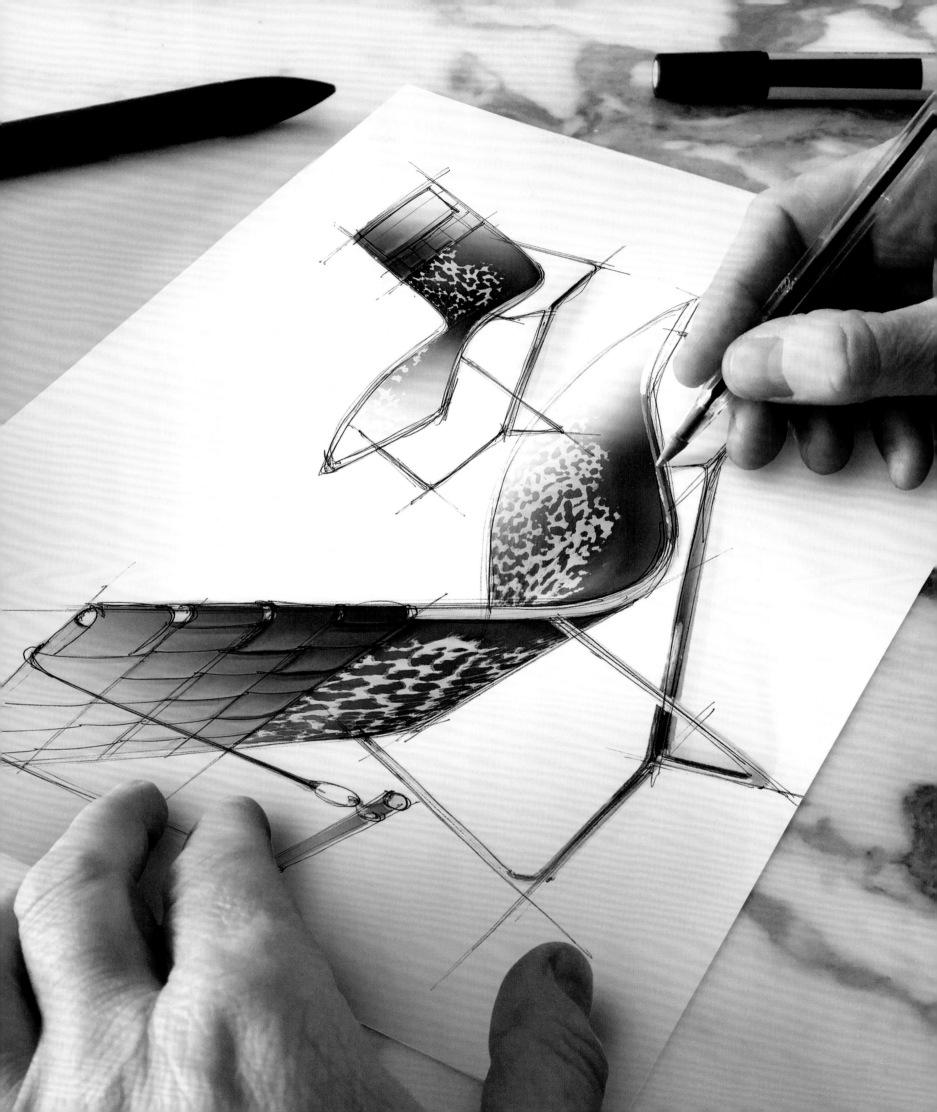

# PART 1

# EVEN FISH HAVE NICE CLOTHES

When Roberto Cavalli—"the artist of fashion"—began designing, it was nature that relentlessly took his breath away. He began to see flora and fauna as the subjects of an almost divine designer: as he famously revealed to *Vogue* in 2011, "God is really the best designer, so I started to copy God." For Cavalli, God became his collaborator, and sinuous serpents, delicate roses, and ravenous tigers began appearing in his collections. More recently, under the direction of current creative director Fausto Puglisi, animal prints and lengths of supple leather have found themselves studded with bronze talons and figurative animalier designs that push the imagery to further evoke the wild and organic genius of natural creation.

In Italian, "collaboration" is referred to as *lavoro di quattro mani*—a work of four hands—and is an essential part of creating objects of great beauty and exceptional quality. Cavalli has been embracing its collaboration with Mother Nature, be it God or otherwise, since its first runway show in 1972, harnessing the organic lines and unexpected color combinations that match black with ocher, pink with orange, and chartreuse with violet—seemingly improbable pairings that are somehow at home on a towering giraffe, kaleidoscopic bird of paradise, or scuttling lizard. Cavalli Home has since been inspired by the clothes that pre-date it to create pieces that mimic the beautiful "dress" of nature by enlisting the help of some of the finest artisans across Italy, utilizing skills passed down through the generations.

The brand's glass and metal works, nestled in the rugged hills close to Siena, realizes Cavalli's visionary designs to produce statement homewares ranging from vessels resembling tortoiseshell and freeform organic vases to golden serpentine forks and lattice-work goblets. And the same care and attention is devoted to their sumptuous linens, radiant tiles, hand-hewn furniture, wild wallpaper ... each the result of a *lavoro di quattro mani* that maximizes the input of skilled craftspeople to ensure that every piece is made *better*. The trademark "Made in Italy" certification often to be found on Cavalli's products is testament to their spirit of collaboration and unwavering pursuit of the ultimate in luxury Italian design.

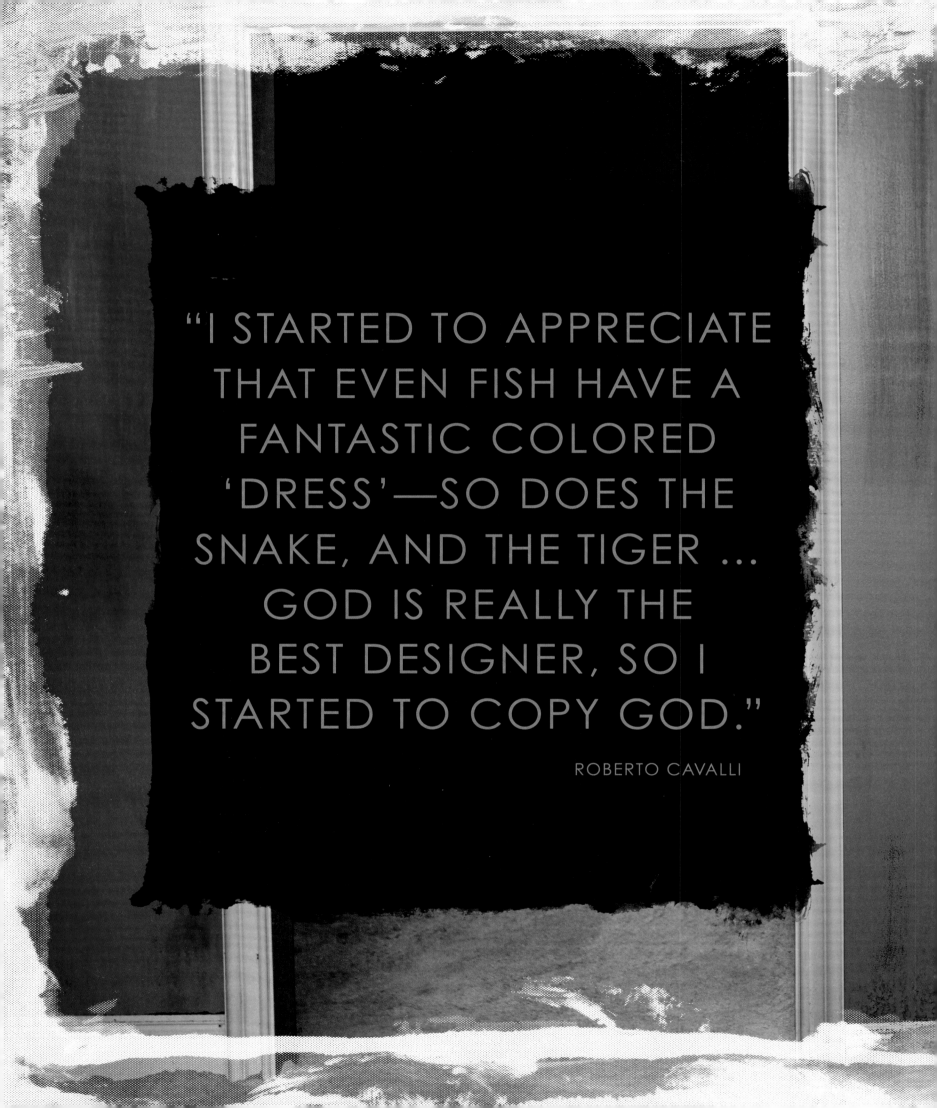

"I STARTED TO APPRECIATE THAT EVEN FISH HAVE A FANTASTIC COLORED 'DRESS'—SO DOES THE SNAKE, AND THE TIGER ... GOD IS REALLY THE BEST DESIGNER, SO I STARTED TO COPY GOD."

ROBERTO CAVALLI

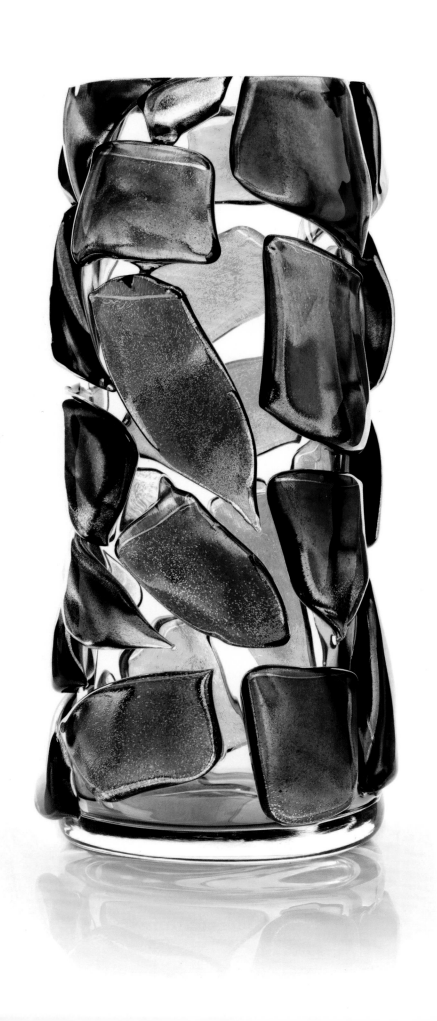

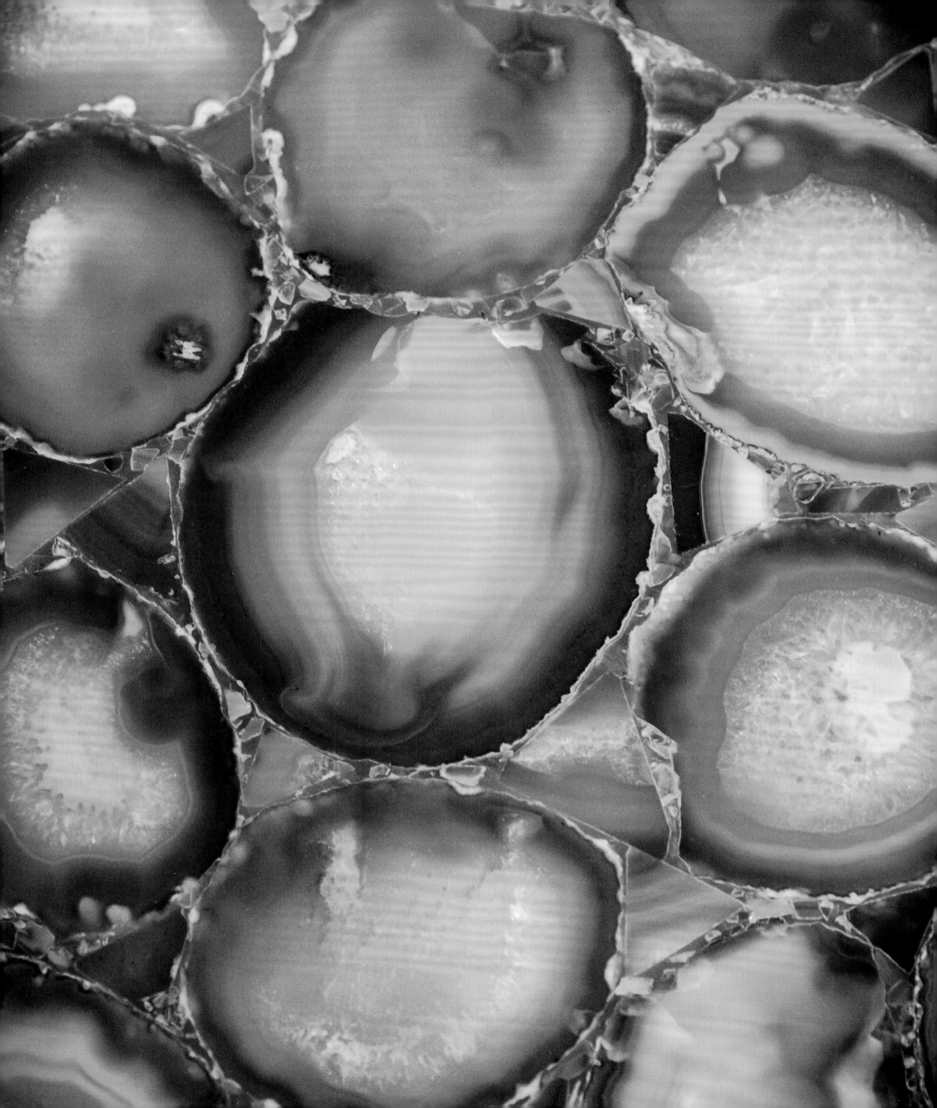

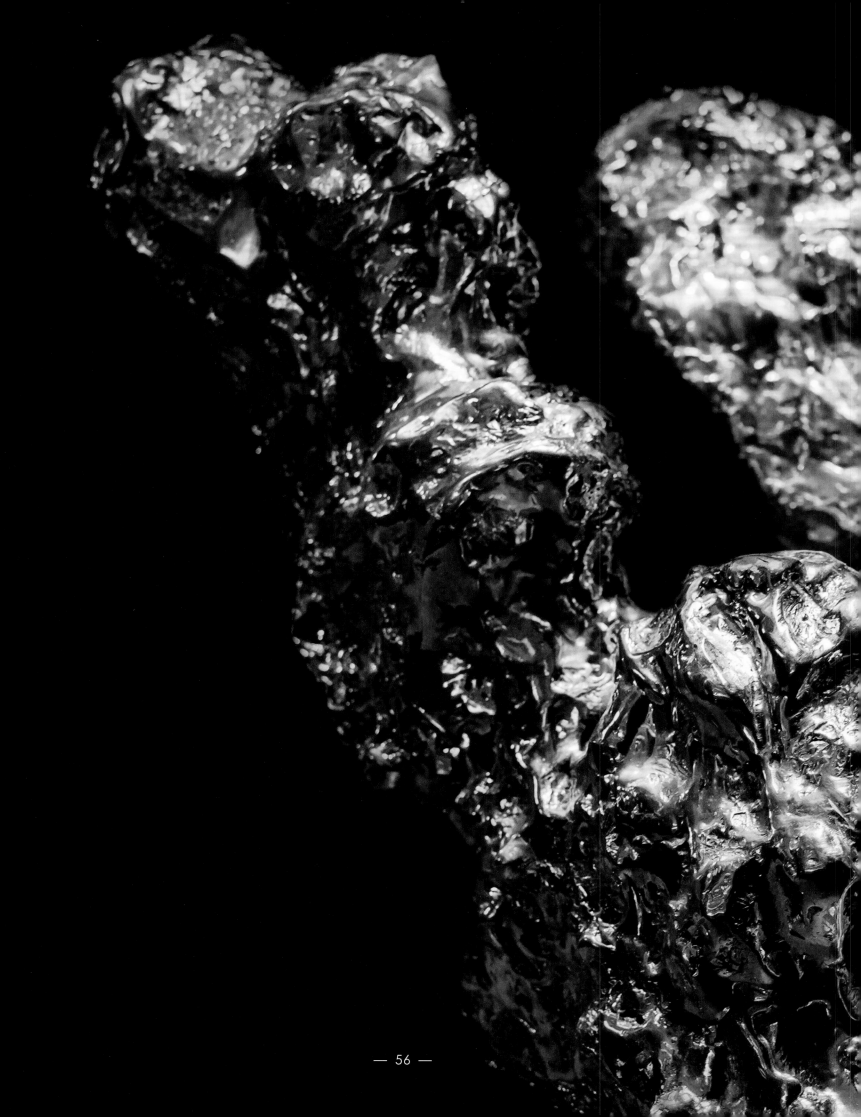

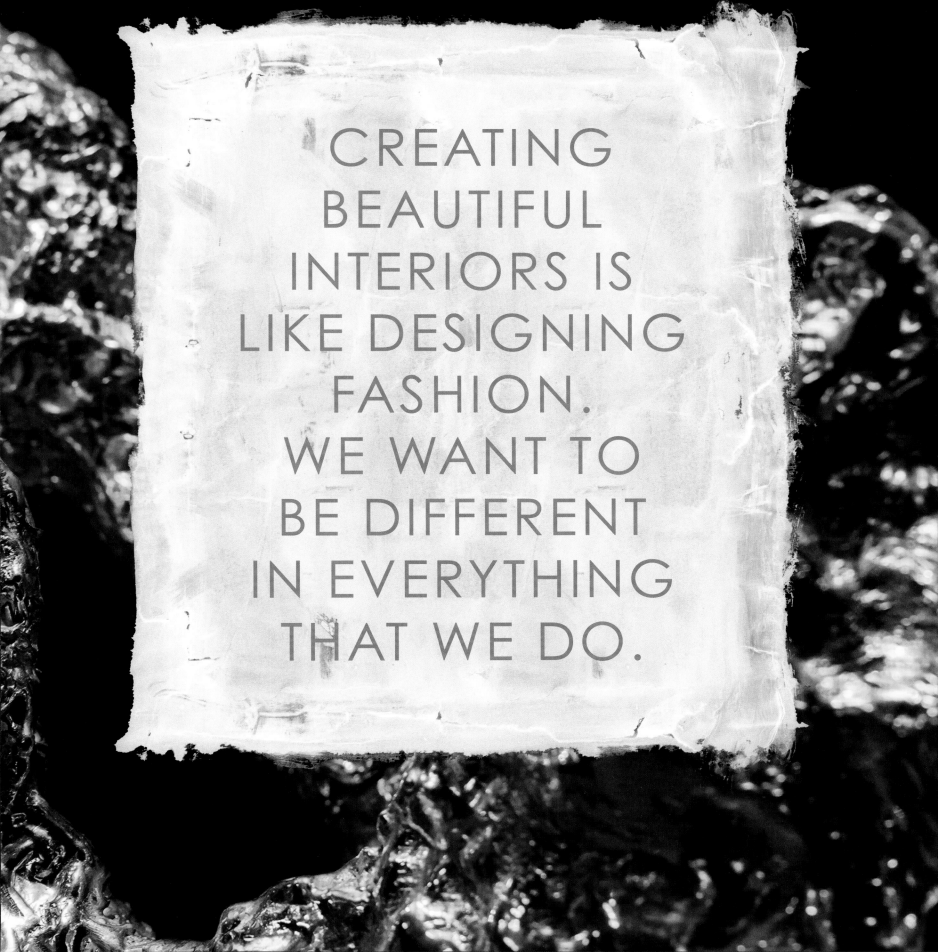

CREATING
BEAUTIFUL
INTERIORS IS
LIKE DESIGNING
FASHION.
WE WANT TO
BE DIFFERENT
IN EVERYTHING
THAT WE DO.

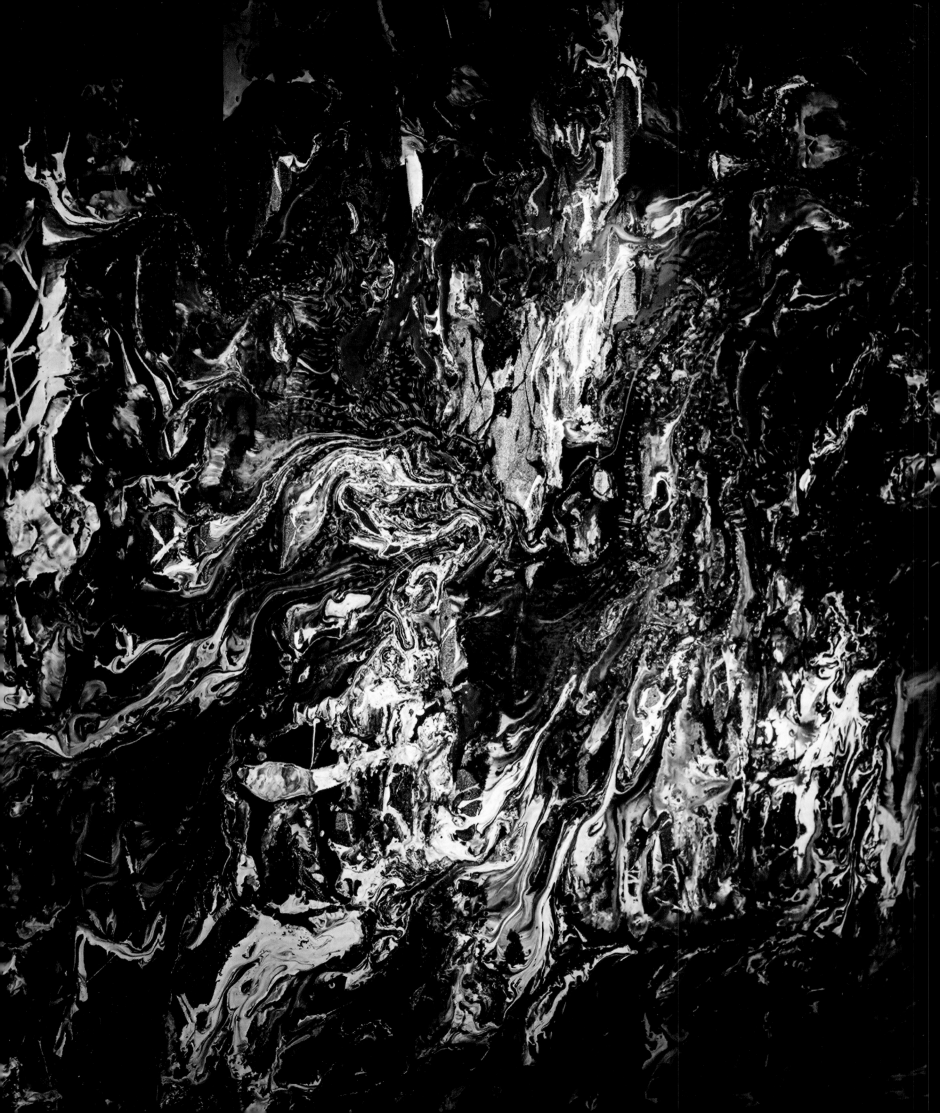

# PART 2

# COUNTRYSIDE IN *CITTÀ*

When the company started as a small business in Florence, Roberto Cavalli imbued not just each collection, but also the company itself, with his joie de vivre. "My lifestyle is always a meeting of passions," Cavalli revealed, when asked about his inspiration for creating the Cavalli Home line—something that remains true to the brand today. Living in the Florentine hills, yet still close to the city's heart, he was able to combine urban cosmopolitan influences with the raw wildness of the countryside in what was to become the brand's trademark signature style.

A home does not come alive until it is inhabited. For Cavalli's founders, Roberto and Eva, this included a wolfhound named Lupo, a monkey named Mac, numerous parrots, a flower and vegetable garden, and, of course, their children. For Casa Cavalli, this blend is essential: finding the place where the countryside and the city come together, welcoming nature indoors and merging the artificial with the organic, infusing the home with pieces that remind us of that connection.

As Cavalli's archive of patterns and prints has grown over the years, Cavalli Home has been able to revive some of the brand's most beloved designs and catapult them into a new and exciting dimension. While the beauty of fashion is in its immediacy, each piece in the Home line is produced over the course of a number of years, rather than just for one season, and is made with the skill and craftsmanship that ensures a timeless longevity in any home, be it a yacht, rural villa, or city-center apartment.

Bold. Abstract. Iconic. Wild. Cavalli Home combines city and countryside to make a true statement in home decor.

# LIFE IS A MEETING OF PASSIONS.

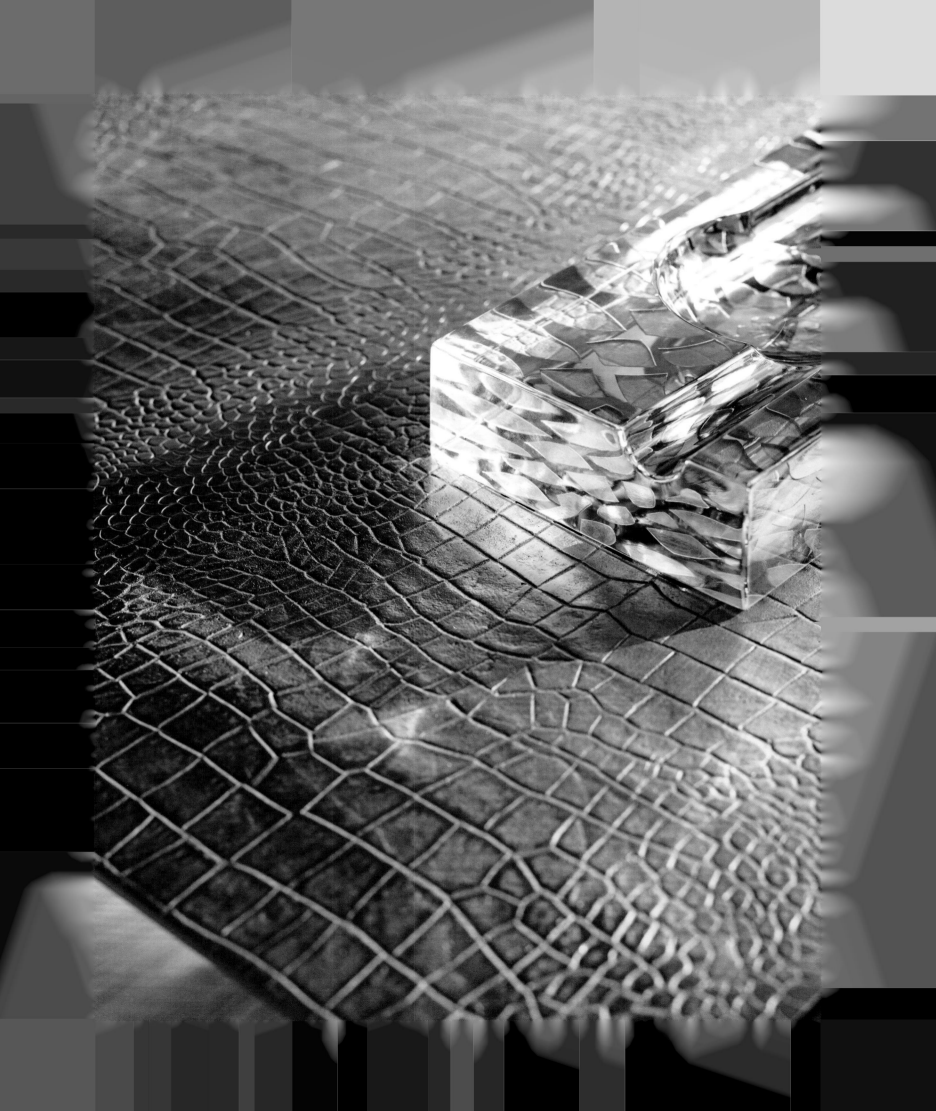

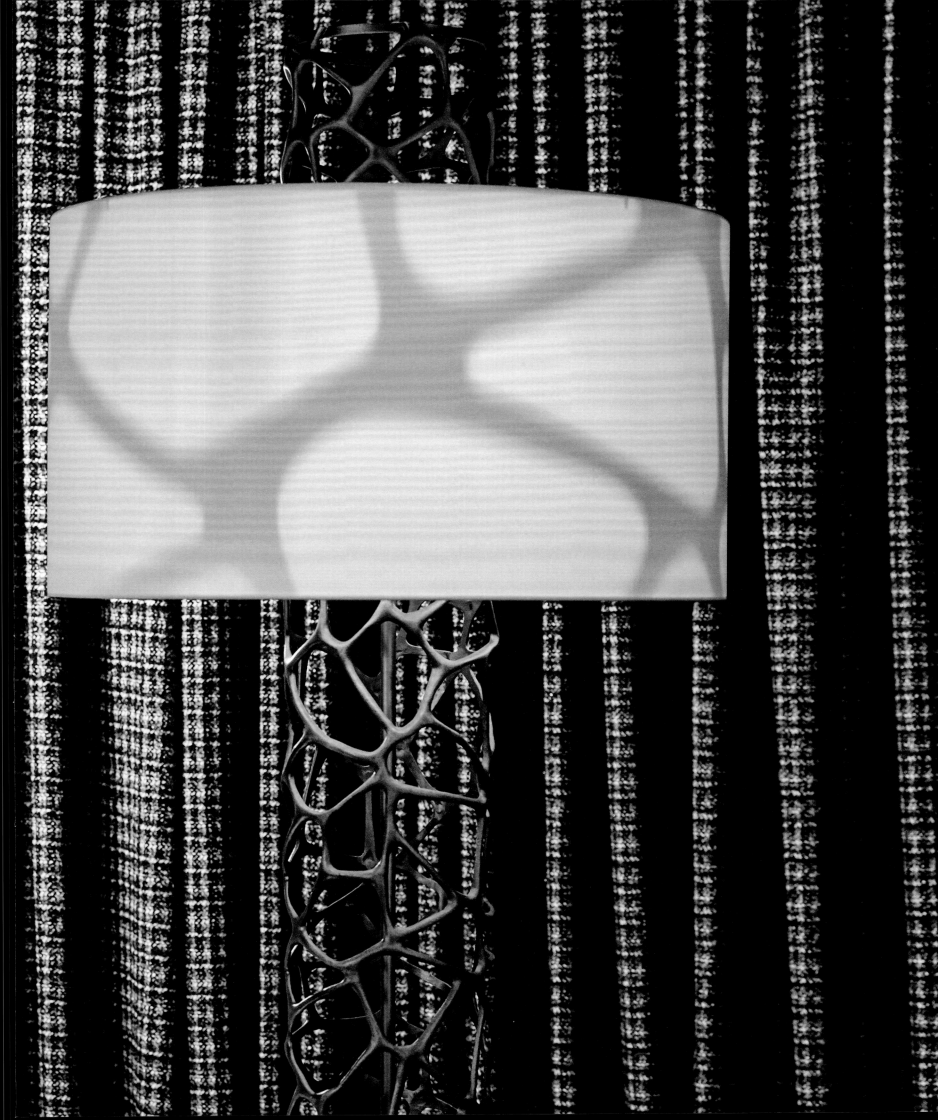

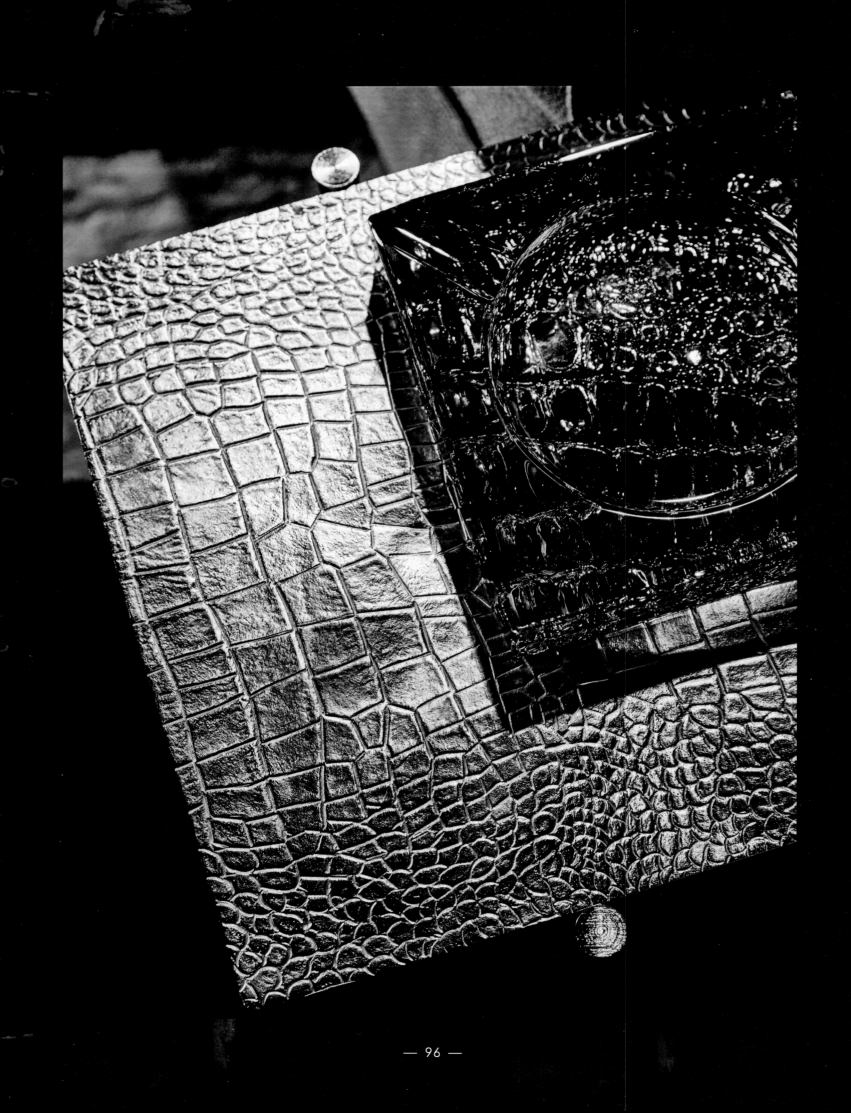

"MORE THAN A FASHION DESIGNER, I AM AN ARTIST OF FASHION."

ROBERTO CAVALLI

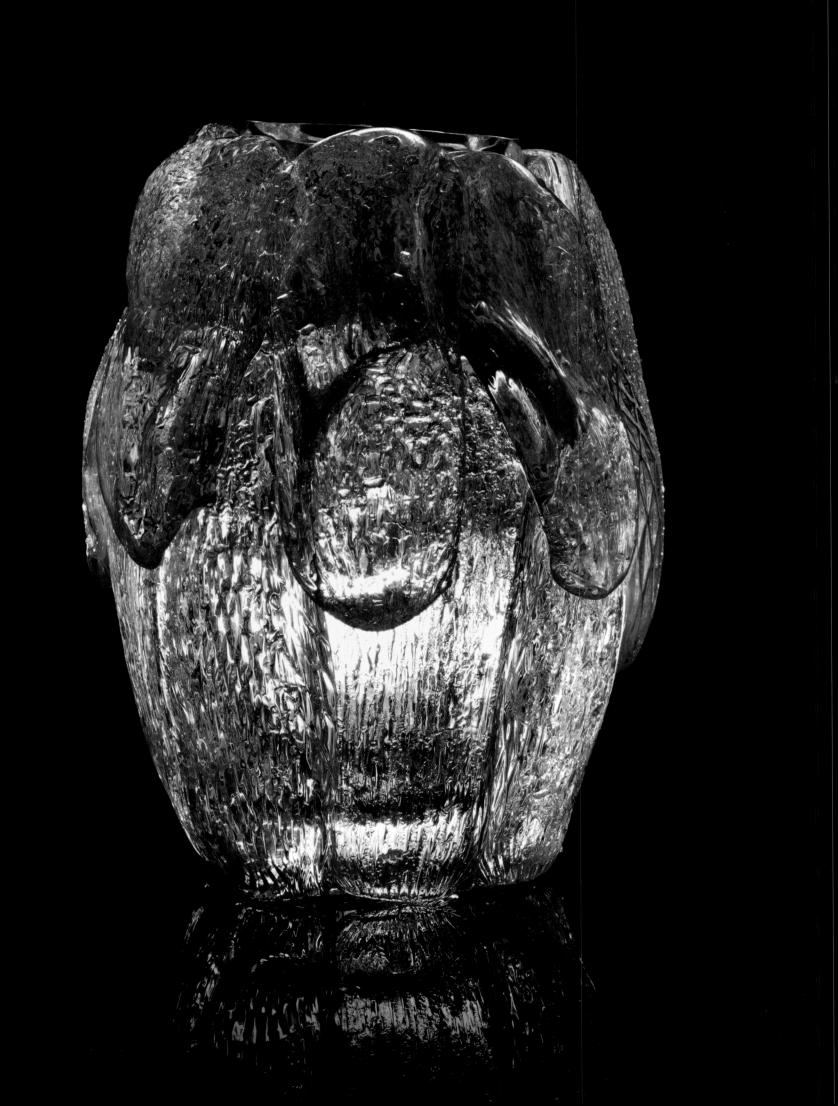

# PART 3

# BRINGING THE WILD

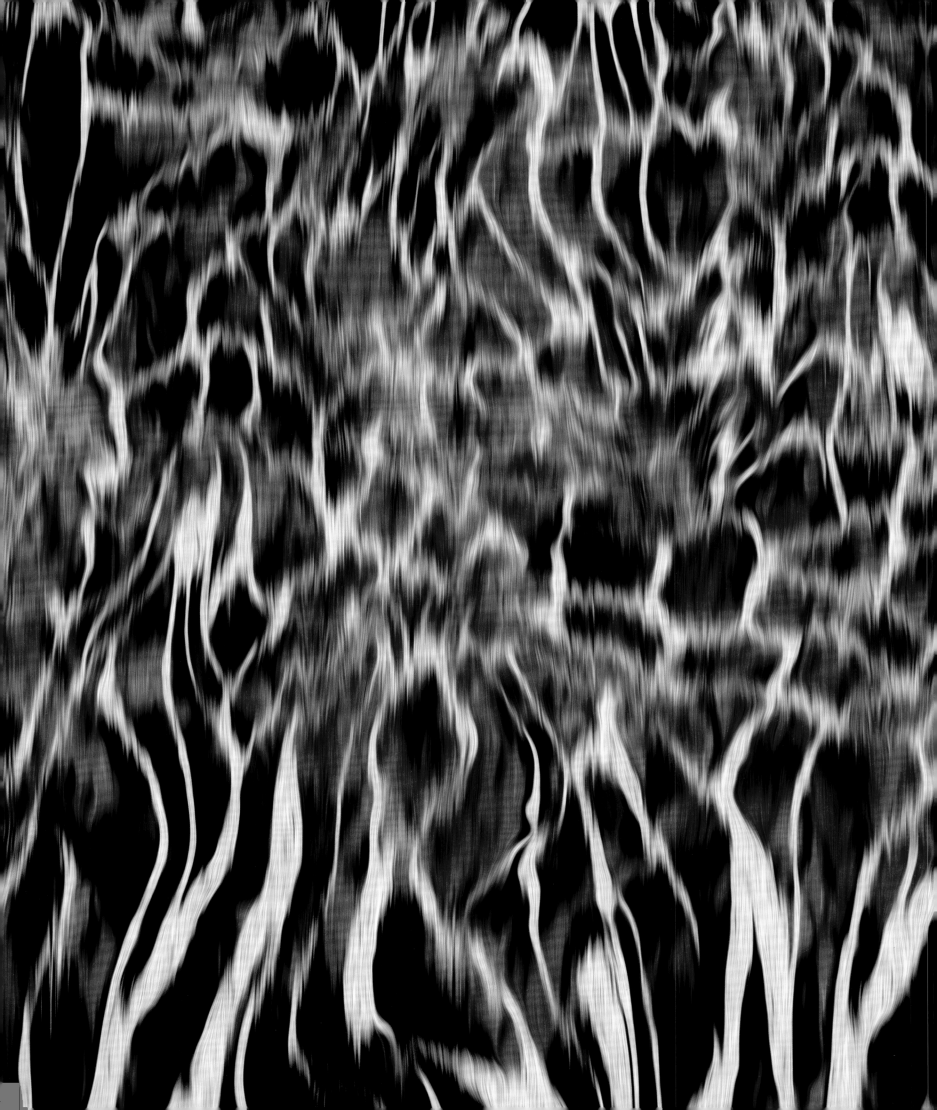

# BE YOURSELF. BE CAVALLI. BE UNIQUE.

To wear and live with Cavalli is to be unique, to run free, to feel *special*. In the Cavalli ethos, style is about revealing an inner beauty, which the pieces in these collections effortlessly achieve by evoking the wild, raw, independent natural world.

Renowned across the globe as the design world's premier atelier in animal prints and patterns, from leopard-print gilets and tiger-stripe cocktail dresses to snakeskin-patterned tableware and zebra-print chairs, Maison Cavalli leads the way in bringing a taste of wild luxury to our closets and homes. Inspired by Roberto Cavalli's own travels to exotic places, the label's bold and glamorous animal-print designs tap into a daring, audacious energy that heightens emotions and desire, allowing us to radiate confidence by creating a second skin, and in so doing reveal inner aspects of ourselves—our anima—to the world.

The Cavalli persona is a constellation of spirit animals—a wild and untamed aesthetic that allows us at once to become objects of desire and apex predators, eager to push the boundaries and break free. Sensual and sumptuous, fierce and unbridled, Cavalli's signature animalier style tempts us to take a walk on the wild side and unleash the animal within.

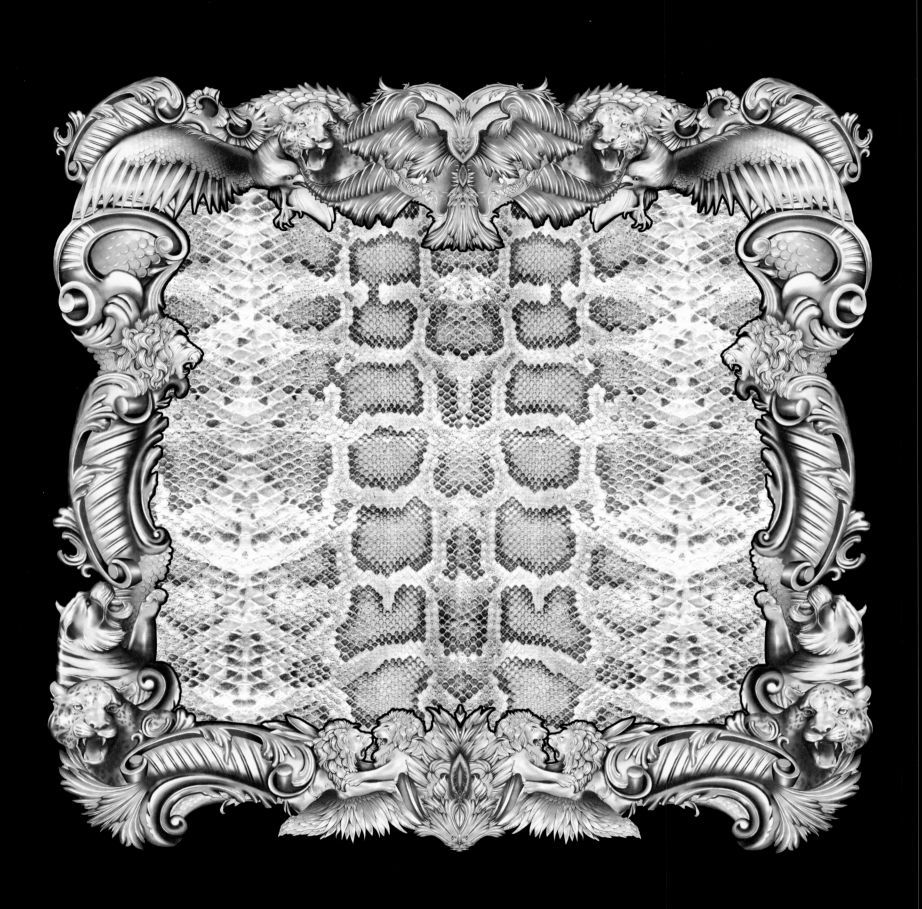

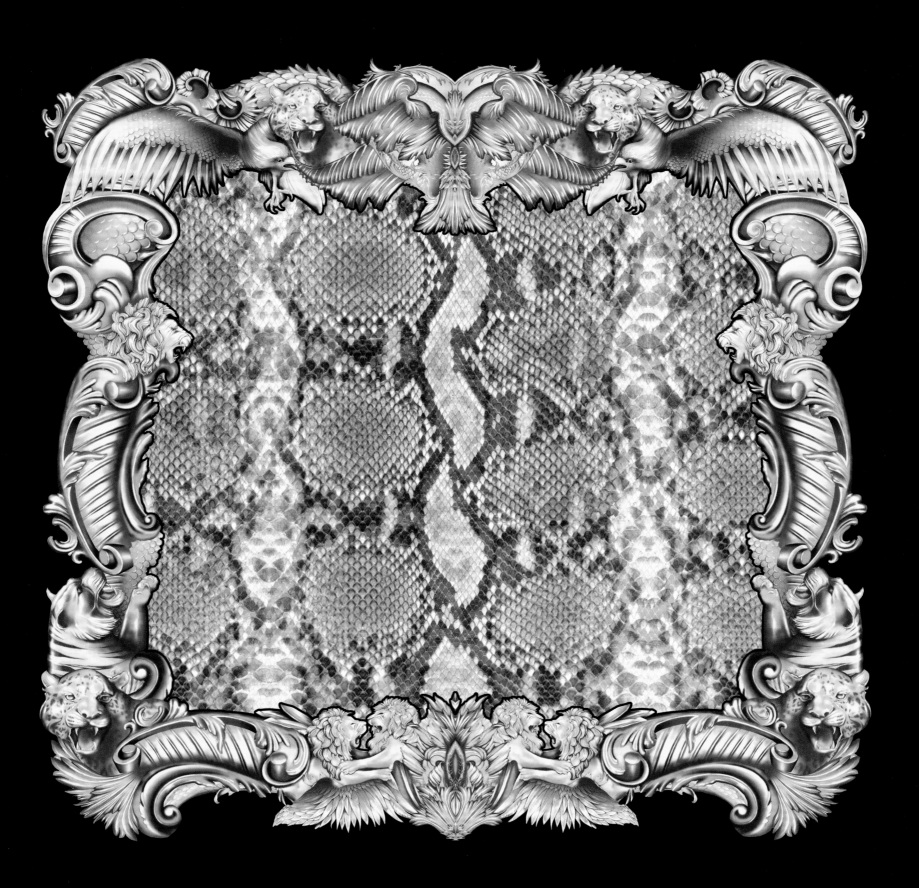

ANIMAL PRINT
MAKES
EVERYTHING
MORE SEXY.

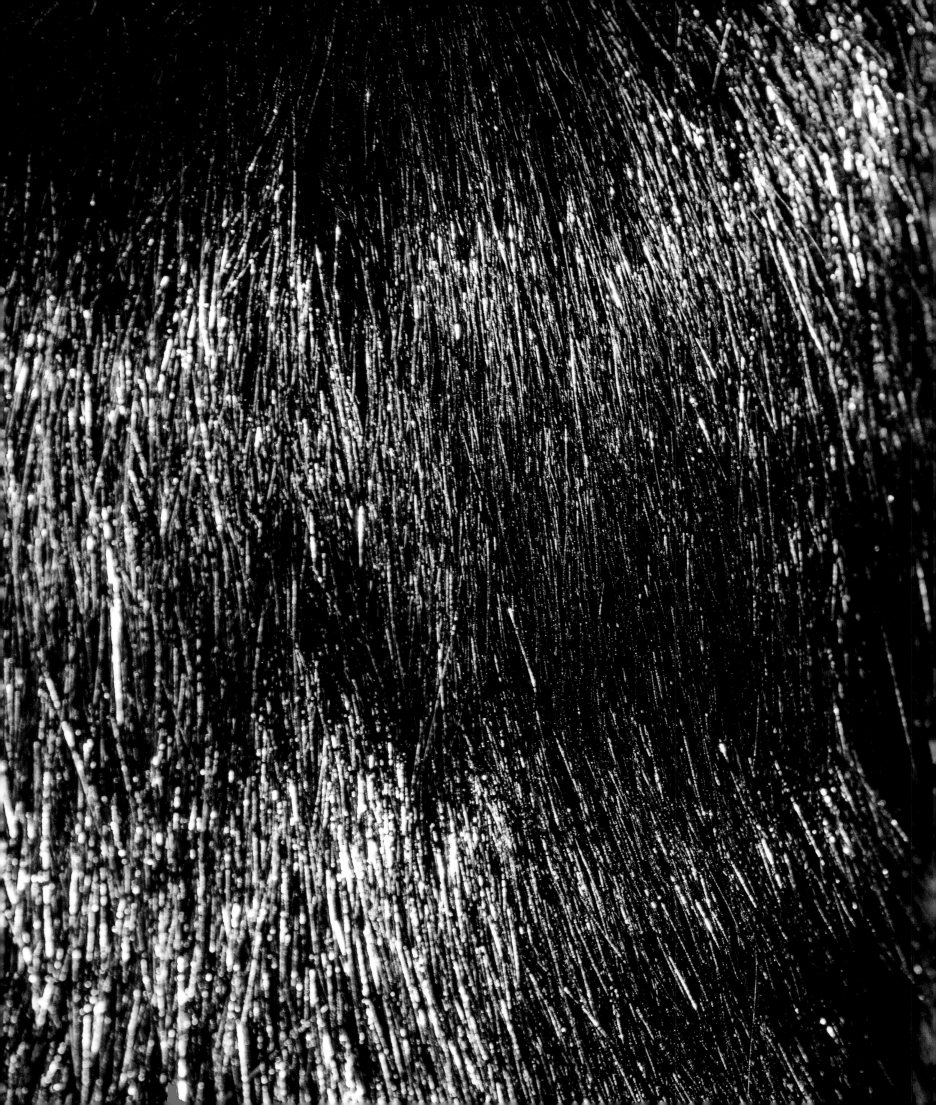

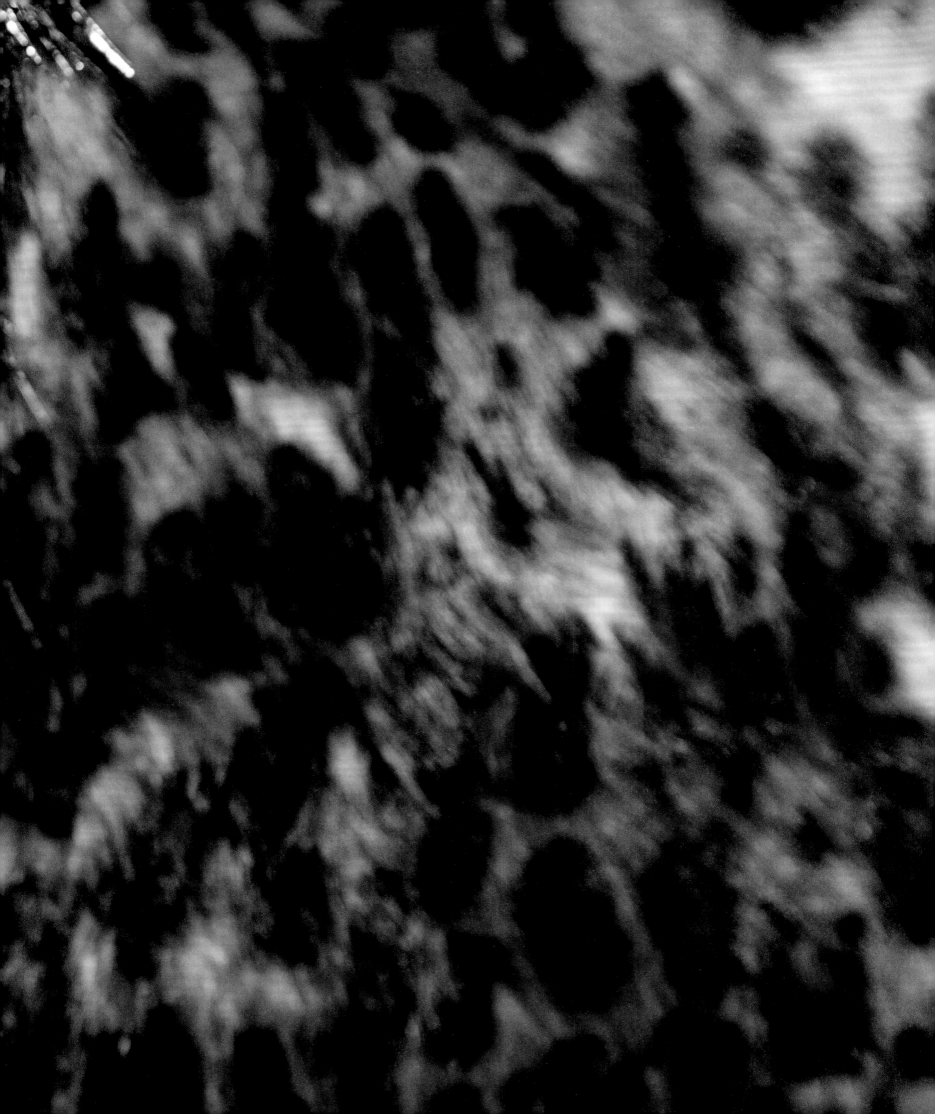

Real beauty is inside. Everyone has it—and clothes have the power to unlock it.

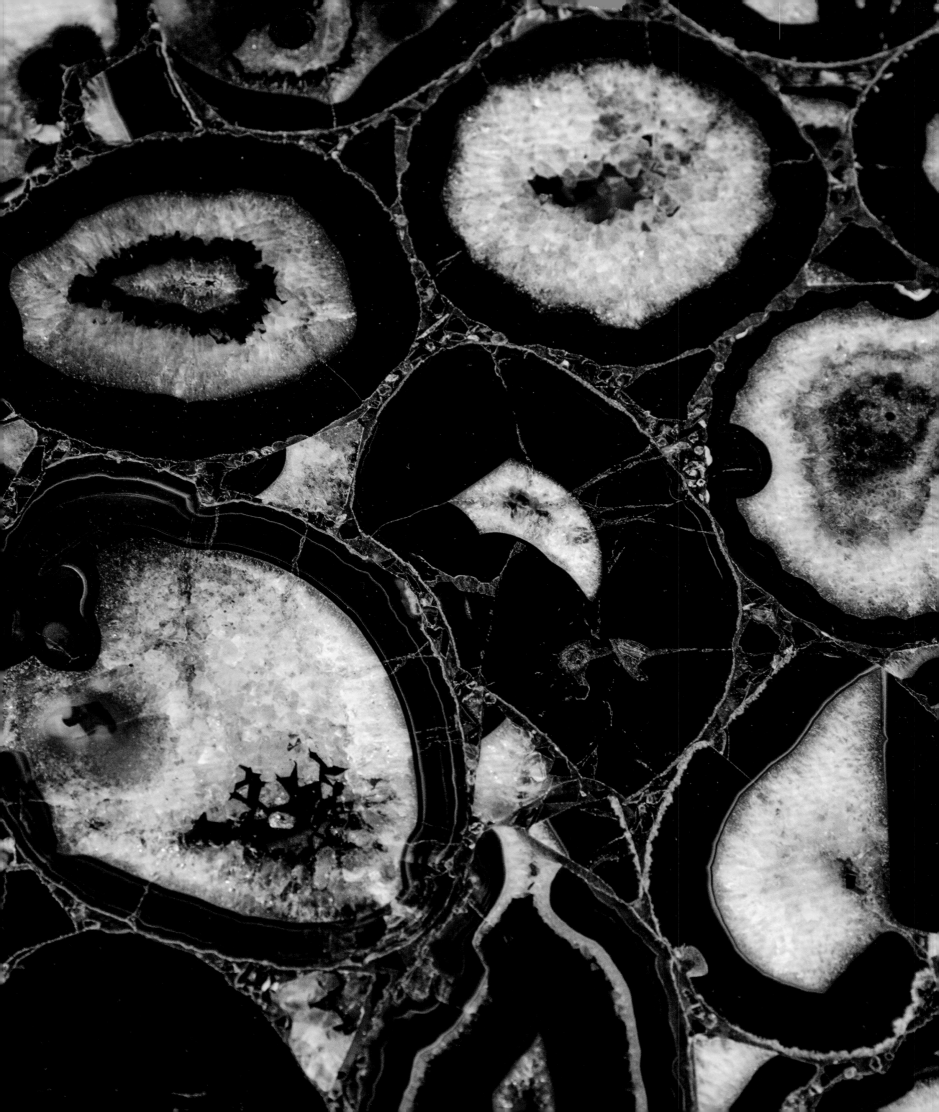

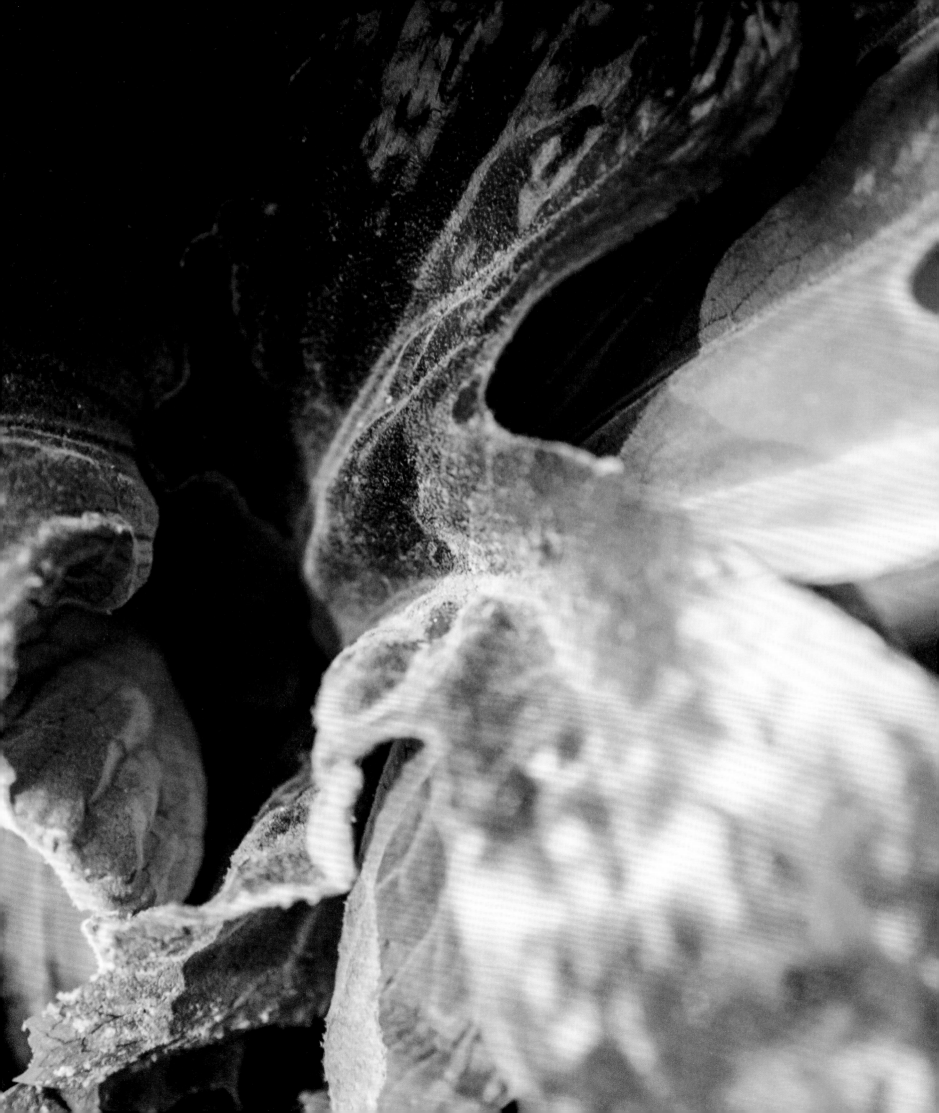

# PART 4

# ADDING *FRIZZANTE* AT HOME

Italian design, especially Roberto Cavalli, embraces life. Whether monochromatic or awash with bright colors, it has an easy notoriety that exudes confidence and is nonchalantly recognizable. Ten years ago, when the Roberto Cavalli Home line was launched, the company brought the baroque and immersive style of their fashion line to a whole range of objects and interior decor. Pieces filled with beauty and adventure make up a collection that is decadent, pleasurable, and brimming with life. Through collaborating with the best of Italian artisans, the Cavalli Home collection has come to reside in the same world as their haute couture: you know a Cavalli piece when you see it.

Cavalli has always embraced the exuberant side of life, be it a pair of jeans stamped with "Queen of Sicily" leopard print and a silk overcoat covered in "Flower Felix" or rich Italian-spun cotton lynx bedsheets and sensual bamboo-silk jaguar carpet. A room that has been dressed in Cavalli is truly memorable: luxurious layers blend together seamlessly to create a signature look that oozes glamour and style. Feather-trimmed or appliqué-gilded, Cavalli decor is not shy. Even just a touch of Cavalli in an otherwise restrained room brings that bit of sparkle and ties a look together—a stripe of tiger wallpaper, perhaps, or splash of "Rock Symphony" tiles.

Fashion and style are about more than being tasteful. They are about celebrating life and the bringing together of people—a way to show off our independence and revel in shared experience. Cavalli Home is that spritz of *frizzante* that brightens up our lives. With Roberto Cavalli, we *are* the party, enjoying the delicious excess of the wild world.

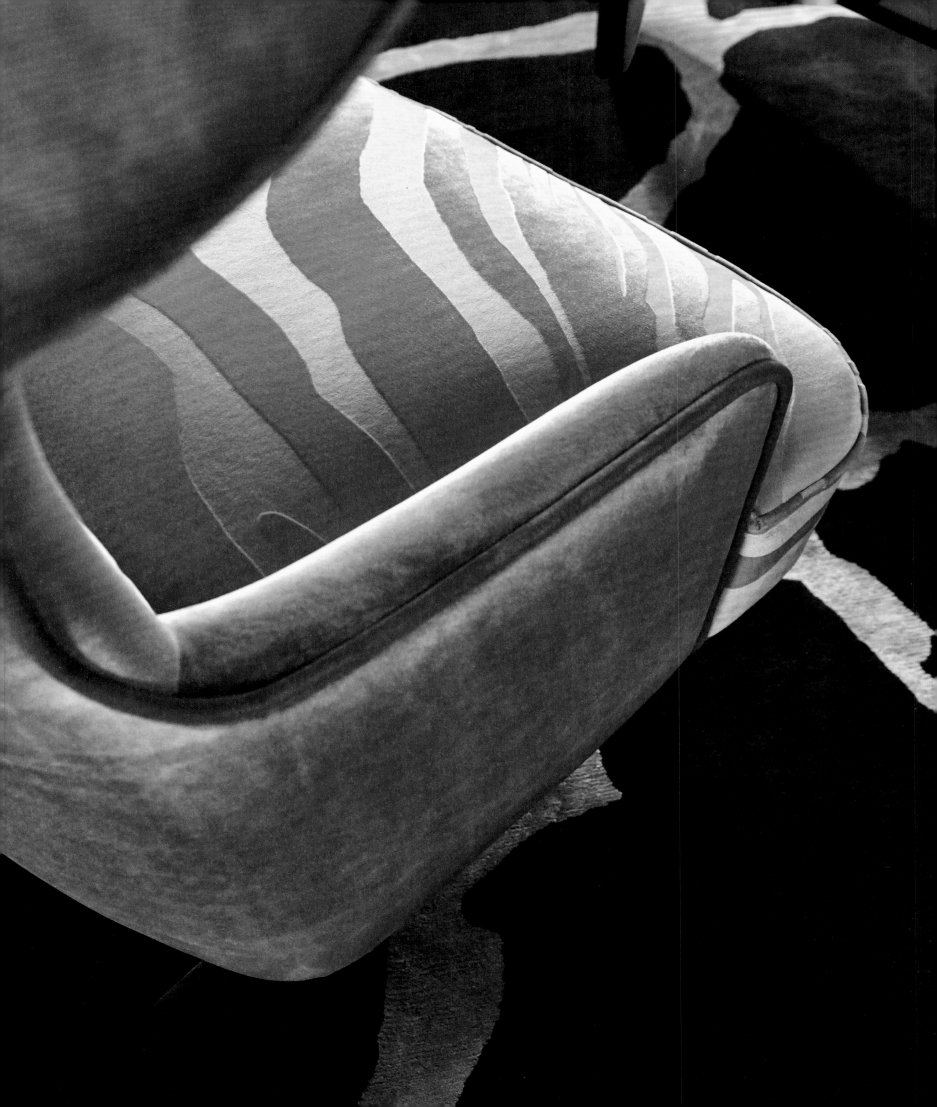

"MISSING
THE PARTY?
HOW CAN I
MISS THE PARTY?

I AM THE PARTY!"

ROBERTO CAVALLI

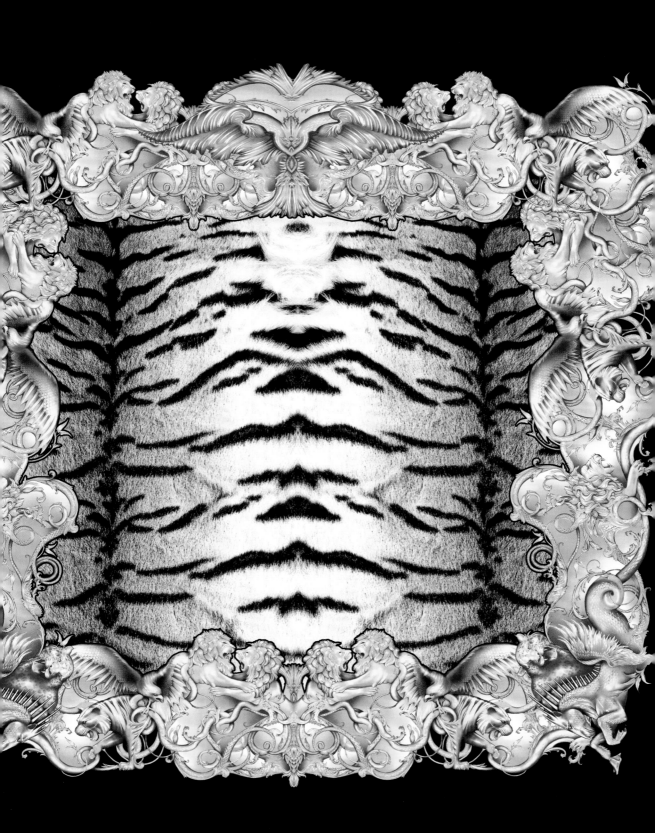

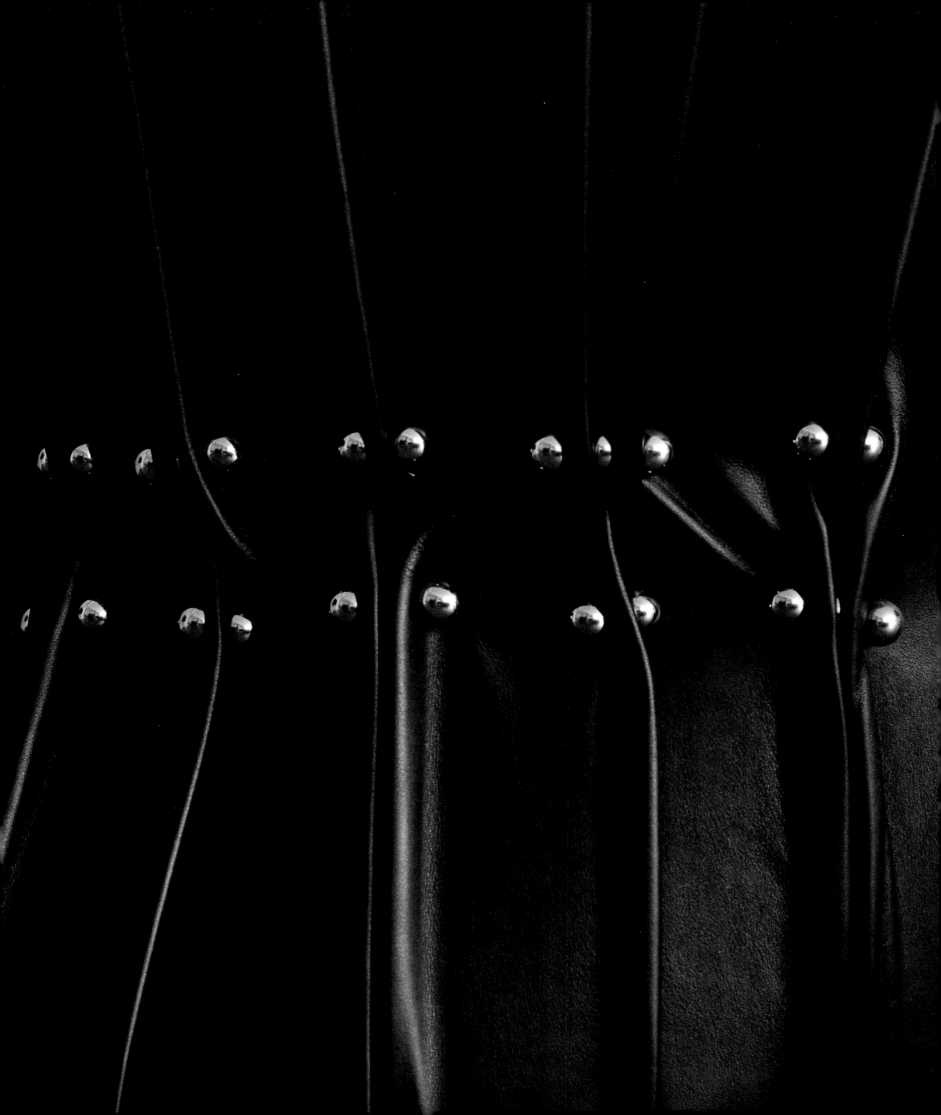

# THERE IS NO SUCH THING AS TOO MUCH!

# PART 5

# THE POWER
# OF BLACK
# AND WHITE

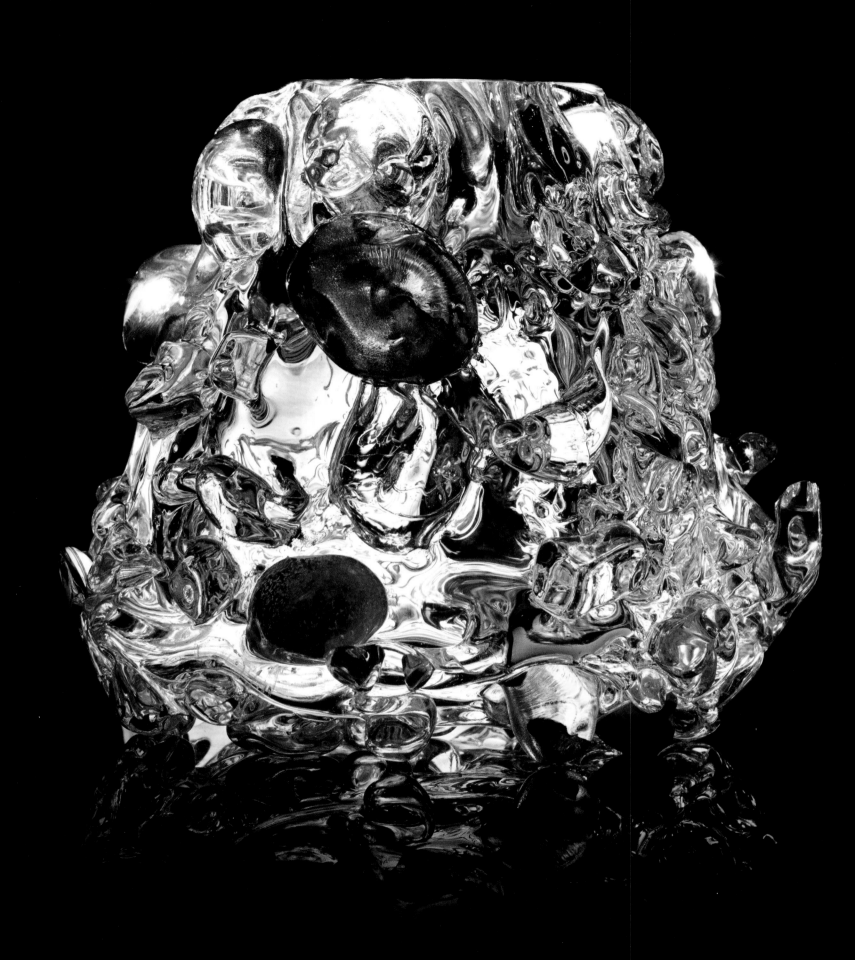

Nature, our perennial font of inspiration, has amazing ways of painting with color. But the more we look, the more we can see that it isn't the flash of red or swath of orange that makes a design sing, but the rich blacks and creamy whites that give color its contrast and truly set it off. It takes a dash of black or white to really make color come to life, be it a bursting peony flecked with pink and ecru, or a leopard whose spots make its ocher dazzling and desirable.

For the artist, color begins with the rendering of raw materials: grinding the azure lapis stone into a deep-blue powder, or harvesting marigolds for their vibrant yellow. But the metamorphosis into art comes when these pigments are transferred to the palette, ready to be mixed into unique tones, tinted with white and shaded with black.

As a painter and textile designer, it was Roberto Cavalli's play of light and shadow —finding color between black and white—and his trademark use of patchwork that first made the fashion house stand out, and still defines the brand to this day. Throughout the company's fifty years, and the Home line's first decade, bold color has been a touchstone of Roberto Cavalli. The dense jungle scenes and tiger stripes in Cavalli prints harness the rich colors that saturate our natural world.

In spaces overwhelmed with brilliant whites and inky blacks, the bold colors in individual products, like a gold lamp, red throw pillow, or emerald vase, stand out even more. Life in black and white reminds us that an absence of pigment, and a collage of light and dark, can accentuate and define colors and shapes to striking effect.

Roberto Cavalli is always different, and the company's designs often lead with lush colors in unusual combinations. But it is that touch of black and flash of white that makes a pattern a true original.

FASHION
THAT IS
NOT CRAZY
IS NOT
FASHION.

THE MOST
IMPORTANT
LUXURY TO
HAVE IS
FREEDOM.

# IT'S ABOUT
# FINDING JOY

There is an art to finding joy, and in the glamorous world of Cavalli it starts with dressing up. Getting ready to go out or preparing to host an evening at home is a form of therapy—the promise of shared moments filled with excitement, an exchange of ideas, and a sense of community. Be it draping yourself in jewels, laying the table, or staging a room, these acts spark an energy—the seeds of new possibilities that lie ahead.

When Cavalli opened its first shop in St. Tropez in 1972, the focus was on fabric, prints, and hand-stitched leather pieces. Under the helm of founder Roberto Cavalli, flowing dresses and intricately embellished denim entwined the story of "dressing up" with the Cavalli spirit. And, as the brand continued to evolve, something magical happened when Cavalli began making jewelry: the lightness that had always existed with Cavalli fabrics was strengthened by the gold, silver, cloisonné enamel, and hard stones of the Cavalli jewels. It was a landmark moment, and the point when Cavalli transformed from a label into an ethos.

In Italian, the word *gioia* means both "jewel" and "joy." The two meanings are interchangeable and, for Italians, that bit of "bling" is a manifestation of joyfulness. This joy of jewelry, in many ways, led to Cavalli Home, which strives to create an ambience for leisure and pleasure, with irresistibly sumptuous pieces that allow lovers of luxury to further explore the joyful and sensual delights of the home.

From teacups and tumblers to vases and plates, Cavalli tableware offers the lure of a journey filled with mystery and charm, as characterized by Cavalli's trademark animalier designs and botanical motifs. Objects are created with a glamorous and exotic soul and give life to the luxurious *art de la table*. Dressing a table is always personal; in Italy, where dinners linger into the early hours, punctuated by courses of few but fine ingredients, the table becomes a theater for laughter, conversation, and love.

Finding joy for Cavalli is about finding the jewels of life, whether precious objects to dress up any occasion or simply moments to treasure spent with loved ones and friends.

THE TABLE
IS A THEATER
FOR LAUGHTER,
CONVERSATION,
AND LOVE.

This wonderful world in which we were born, filled with colors, shapes, and joy, is our ultimate source of inspiration!

# PART 7

# EMBRACING HISTORY WITH NEW EXCITEMENT

# "Okay, let's rewind. Let's write a new book. This is a preface."

In a world filled with walls and divisions, "exclusivity" is the luxury of mixing different kinds of people together—breaking down barriers in a colorful and democratic way, and merging diverse cultures, experiences, roots. This is the new Cavalli for me.

I called my first collection for Roberto Cavalli "Collection Zero." I was designing in the middle of the pandemic—in this separation between the past and the future, when Italy, my home, was suffering. It was born in the liminal moment when the whole world was frozen, and I wanted to create a strong yet neutral Cavalli. A "baseline." I layered desert and skin tones over jaguar, leopard, and zebra prints, which we styled with aspects of ancient East Asian etching. From here, we could start again, and move forward.

Roberto Cavalli used to say "I am the party"—and he was! He created a brand so full of life, so exciting, it became magnetic. I deeply believe the idea of a party today is somewhere you can find the queen, the king, the royalty of music, alongside the everyday people working as plumbers or bakers. I would go crazy in a static world that is only one thing or the other. The most exciting spaces are where you have a clash of cultures. By being open, we have rediscovered the party.

Several years ago, one of my bespoke creations was acquired by the Victoria and Albert Museum in London. When a piece joins a permanent collection, it becomes like a painting or a statue. This is the spirit of haute couture—a work that straddles the line between garment and art. This is why designing furniture and objects for the home is not so different from designing a beautiful dress: sometimes a piece of Cavalli is that jewel that lives in your wardrobe to be loved and looked at, but rarely worn. I am not interested in "fast fashion," and devote the same level of attention and focus to the design of a chair or lamp as to the next catwalk collection. It is this dedicated approach to craftsmanship—something to be championed— that connects the Cavalli Home line with couture and transports Cavalli's fashion collections to dining tables and living rooms.

"The craftmanship in Italy is something which is extremely connected to the society. It's something that people do because they love it."

For our 2022 Roberto Cavalli Home collection, for example, unveiled at the Salone del Mobile in Milan, I created the "Queen of Cavalli Chair." In collaboration with our artisans—some of the best in Italy—we were able to sculpt from wood this limited-edition signature piece. Inspired by a 16th-century Versailles chair, and upholstered in a variety of bright, electric prints that I designed, this ebonized chair combines a European heritage with an edge of American pop culture. And, by mixing different prints together around a table or in the same room, it becomes a feast for the eyes.

Cavalli is this "feast"—and what the world needs right now. We need joy. We need to dream. This is what I wanted to express with the chairs—and continue expressing with Cavalli in the future. The world will always need a party, but the party has to move with the times.

This is Roberto Cavalli. And the party is home.

FAUSTO PUGLISI
Milan, 2022

# CREDITS

Unless listed below, all images are copyright © Roberto Cavalli S.p.A.

© **Alberto Zanetti:** 6–7, 48, 59, 69, 102–103, 128 (left), 129 (right), 131, 138, 142, 175, 176, 214–215, 232 (inset), 257, 263, 272

© **Annie Leibovitz:** 60–61, 90–91, 94 (inset)

© **Carlo Vigni:** 2–3, 36, 36–37 (center), 104, 105, 196, 200, 201, 250–251 (center), 251

© **Francesco Carrozzini:** 28–29, 46–47, 195, 228–229

© **Giampaolo Sgura:** 21, 43

© **Inez & Vinoodh:** 146, 165 (inset)

© **Jack Waterlot:** 37, 107, 137 (inset), 211, 237

© **Johnny Dufort:** 53, 72–73 (center), 247, 290–291

© **Lorenzo Scaccini:** 8, 10, 15, 22, 24, 25 (background & inset), 27 (inset), 30–31, 33, 34–35 (background), 40, 41, 42, 42–43 (center), 44, 45, 50, 52, 54, 55, 64, 66–67, 68, 70–71, 72, 76–77, 79, 80, 81, 82, 83, 86 (inset), 88–89, 95, 96, 106, 106–107 (center), 125, 134–135, 139, 140, 143, 146–147 (center), 150, 151, 160–161 (center), 166, 167, 168, 190, 192–193, 210, 212, 222–223, 224–225, 226, 227, 230, 230–231 (center), 234, 238, 240–241, 242, 243 (inset), 244, 245, 246, 246–247 (center), 250, 254–255, 264–265, 267, 277, 278–279, 280, 281, 283, 284, 286, 287, 288, 289, 296

© **Max Vadukul:** 87, 121, 126–127, 128–129 (center), 132, 292

© **Max Zambelli:** 68–69 (center), 84, 85, 97, 100, 101, 133, 144, 178, 179, 182, 183, 184–185, 188, 189, 208, 209, 233, 266, 269

© **Mert & Marcus:** 109, 112–113, 152–153, 173 (inset), 181 (inset), 199 (inset)

© **Morelli Brothers:** 155

© **Silvio Macchi:** 16, 220, 221, 293, 304

© **Tim Walker:** 78, 204

© **Zoë Ghertner:** 63, 73, 145 (inset), 219, 276 (inset)

# roberto cavalli
## HOME

### INTERIORS
www.onirogroup.it

### LINEN
www.mirabellocarrara.it

### LUXURY TABLEWARE
www.arnolfodicambio.com

### LUXURY TILES
www.ricchetti-group.com

### WALLPAPER
www.emilianaparati.com

*Special thanks*
*Enrico Genevois, Franco Mariotti*

PUBLISHERS
Beatrice Vincenzini, Mark Magowan & Francesco Venturi

Distributed in North America by Abrams Books
Distributed in the UK, and rest of the world, by Thames & Hudson

ISBN: 978-0-86565-422-8

WRITER  Christopher Garis
EDITOR  Tessa Monina
PRODUCTION DIRECTOR  Jim Spivey
ART DIRECTOR  Roger Barnard
DESIGNER  Peter Dawson, www.gradedesign.com

Library of Congress Cataloging-in-Publication Data
available upon request

Printed and bound in Italy at Elcograf.

FIRST PRINTING